Good Showing

The new exhibitor's guide to dog showing and the showring

Peggy Grayson

Many people who own a pedigree dog have a desire to enter it for a show but do not know how to set about the task. This book sets out in detail the first steps to a showing career, which may just prove a pleasant pastime, but can lead to the challenging world of the championship show and a lifetime's dedication to breeding and exhibiting.

Contents

The book has been colour coded to help you find relevant sections of illustrations. The colours below correspond to coloured tabs at the top left and right of each page. To find the section you want, simply look for the matching coloured tab.

Acknowledgements

The author would like to thank the following exhibitors and photographers who have helped with the illustrations for this book.

Miss A Roslin Williams
Sharkey
Mrs M Micklewright
Mr and Mrs Higgins
Mrs Deanne Crane
Robert Smith
Carol Ann Johnson
and Angela Begg for the drawings

Acknowledgements also to the following firms whose products are illustrated:

Accolade Leathercraft (show slips)
Snooze and Snack (cages and bowls)
Luxway Beacon Canine Supplies (grooming equipment)

Foreword

More and more people are purchasing pedigree dogs and at some time probably half of them will decide to exhibit their acquisitions.

Showing dogs is more than just buying a dog and entering for a show. This book is set out to help the newcomers with the problems likely to be encountered, to give some tips on the best way to go about preparing both the dogs and themselves for the show ring and to answer some of the many questions asked by newcomers to the world of dog shows.

The author, a successsful exhibitor for many years and now an international judge, has spent a lifetime in pedigree dogs and has held official positions in various breeds and general canine societies.

The advice given is based on personal experience and offered as a guide to exhibitors of the immediate present and future, not only to help newcomers to enjoy their show going and (hopefully) to achieve a measure of success, but also to encourage a responsible attitude to shows and showing.

First Steps

There are many reasons why people decide they want to enter the world of dog shows.

Some come from families where one or more elder members are, or have been, exhibitors.

Some who have bought pedigree dogs are encouraged by friends saying how beautiful the dog is and, 'You ought to show him.' Some watch Crufts Dog Show on television and decide they too would like to be part of such a world.

Some are interested in pedigree livestock, breeding, rearing and ultimately showing stock that is home-produced. Such people hope to improve and influence their breed for the future, to the benefit of those who follow.

Some just like dogs and want an interesting hobby that will involve their dogs. They have some spare time and cash and enjoy the thrill of competition. Yet others are just dog lovers who enjoy showing off their dogs and want to meet and make friends with like-minded people.

No-one should take up dog showing hoping to make a profitable business out of it. Showing dogs involves the flow of money in one direction only – outwards! Very few shows give prize money and the most that winning owners can hope to gain, apart from the pleasure of seeing their dogs win, are prize cards and possibly rosettes.

Much of the show scene today is filled with those who keep their dogs as a hobby and show because they enjoy the whole business of caring for, grooming, training and preparing their dogs. They have the benefit of live and loving companions who will keep them fit by constant demands for exercise, and will make friends with like-minded people. If you are 'in dogs', there is no need ever to be lonely or for the days ahead to be empty or dull.

Life becomes even more exciting and the adrenaline flows with the arrival of show schedules and the need to decide which show to attend and which judge to support. When you have filled in and posted the entry form there is a time of pleasurable anticipation as show day draws near. Then there is the thrill of the day itself: loading up the car, settling the dog, the drive, the arrival, the familiar sounds and smells of the venue, friends calling out greetings, news to exchange... Then there's the buzz when your class is called, the excitement as the judge calls you forward to examine your dog, the anxiety in case it does not move or stand as you have trained it to do, the relief when it does, and the heart-stopping moment when the judge deliberates on his or her choices.

Sometimes your dog will be in the winning line and you will feel elated; sometimes it will be left out and you will feel deflated. If you accept that your dog will not be placed every time, that all judges interpret the breed standard in different ways and that the next show might be the lucky one, you are half way to enjoying all that goes on and becoming a liked and accepted member of the dog showing community.

Those who do grouse and grumble because their dogs have not been placed on the day or who make nasty remarks about the judges or winners will soon find themselves branded trouble-makers and will not gain the friendship of the real 'dog folk';

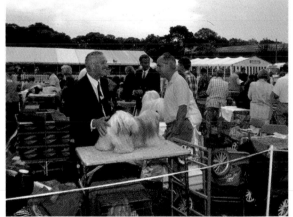

Most established exhibitors will give help and advice to newcomers. Photo: Robert Smith

only of those who behave in a similar manner. No happiness or pleasure lies in that direction. That there will be disasters as well as triumphs must be well understood and taken in good part, or the whole exercise becomes meaningless.

There are various ways of entering the world of dog shows, so it would be as well to give would-be exhibitors an idea of how to go about things.

If you belong to a family who show dogs you will know the score and will not need advice from me; this can be obtained from those with show experience. However, some hints in this and later chapters may put a fresh light on the scene, so do read on!

Because Crufts is the only show that appears on national television, some people think it is the *only* show. How wrong they are! Some 3000 dog shows are held in the British Isles in any one year. Most areas have a canine society and the address of the secretary can usually be obtained from the local library. If not, The Kennel Club will supply the names and addresses of show secretaries in your area. Choose the society that operates nearest to your home and contact the secretary, who will supply you with the date of the next show.

If you attend the show, like the atmosphere and what you see and want to know more, join the society and attend whatever events they have planned. These will be in the form of matches, social gatherings, seminars and so on, and there will possibly be obedience and agility sections, which may attract you more than just exhibiting.

If you already own a pedigree dog, joining one of the clubs catering solely for your breed will provide a means of meeting people in the breed and obtaining valuable information. All breed clubs hold their own shows, so attendance at one of these will give you the chance to see many more specimens of the breed together and to compare the dog at home with the dogs at the show and see whether yours is likely to be successful as a show dog.

Not all pedigree dogs are of show quality, and would-be exhibitors can be spared a great deal of expense and heartache if they recognise this before they decide to go ahead and exhibit. Owning a pedigree dog, however many champions it has in its pedigree, does not mean automatic wins. To avoid disappointment, study the breed and its requirements well before entering the dog at a show.

If you do not yet own a dog but wish to purchase one with a view to showing, again it is wise to learn all you can about the breed by visiting shows and kennels to examine it at close hand. Buy a good breed book and study it. If you are really serious, ring one or two well-known kennels in the breed. Tell the breeders you are interested in owning one of the breed but wish to know more about it before purchase and ask if you may come and see the dogs. The best breeders are only too pleased to show off their dogs to a visitor who is truly interested, and you will find such people immensely helpful.

If you visit a number of kennels before purchase you will soon get to know which breeders are prepared to be helpful in either selling you a suitable puppy or sending you to someone equally reliable who has good stock for sale.

Choosing a puppy that might make the grade is not a job for an amateur. Allow the breeder to indicate which of the puppies for sale is the most likely to succeed. Do not ignore his or her advice and take one that attracts you because it is smaller and cuter than the others, or because it comes up and makes a fuss of you; that's fine if you want a pet but, if you're serious about showing the puppy when it is old enough, take the advice of those who know.

No matter how well bred a puppy may be, or how well reared, it is always a toss up whether it will make the grade. It may grow too big or not grow big enough, have a wrong mouth when the teeth change or develop various other faults. No-one, not even the most experienced of breeders, should guarantee that a puppy of eight to ten weeks will become a show specimen; there are too many imponderables in the keeping and rearing of livestock.

The successful growth and development of the puppy will depend on you: how it is kept, reared, treated and fed. Take advice from whoever sells you the pup, and refer constantly to the best book available on the breed. Do not worry unduly about the puppy or your thoughts will communicate themselves to it and could make it shy or a worrier. Do not be constantly on your veterinary surgeon's doorstep. Apart from the necessary inoculations a young puppy should not need any veterinary attention if it is fed and housed properly. A relaxed, pleasant atmosphere with plenty of play and kind but firm discipline right from puppyhood is essential if the puppy is to grow up to be a well balanced adult who will enjoy its show days as much as you will.

For those who already own a pedigree dog and want to show it, do go and look at the breed at shows. If your dog is not a great specimen of its breed and you still want to show but cannot afford or do not have the space for a dog of better quality, there are plenty of small shows where you and your dog can have great fun. For the bigger events, wait until you can afford to purchase, feed and house another dog of better show quality.

Novices Who Got Lucky

Deanne Crane wanted a Gordon Setter puppy as a pet. The Kennel Club put her in touch with the Gordon Setter Club, who introduced her to successful breeder Mrs Yvonne Horrocks. Deanne chose her puppy from three offered. She had no thought of showing until she and Logan attended ringcraft classes when Logan was ten months old. The family pet has now become Sh Ch Carek Wild Horse, a well-known winner in the breed, which goes to show that novices can be successful if they have a good dog and good advice about presentation and handling. Her photograph here is by Carol Ann Johnson.

In 1982 Ken and Jackie Higgins bought a Bull Terrier bitch puppy through an advertisement in *Exchange & Mart*. Zuki was to be just a pet, but it was suggested she be shown. A second prize at a Bull Terrier Club show started them off and Zuki became Ch Bella Bianca Jackenna, one of the top winners of her day and recipient of the coveted Regent Trophy, the highest award in the breed.

Types of Show

There really is something for everybody in the way of dog shows.

Working or Hunt Terrier Shows

These shows are usually organised by the local hunt supporters' groups and take place at country fairs or similar gatherings. They are not shows in which the dogs are judged for their looks; the dogs are judged solely on whether they are of the type and build that can work. The Kennel Club has special rules for these but, if you own a terrier that comes within the categories scheduled, it is in order to enter.

These shows are slanted at the true working terrier and are usually judged by a Master of Hounds, Hunt Servant, Terrierman or the like, who will look for correct size, fitness, good coats and mouths and keen, alert eyes. There are classes for Jack Russells, Lakelands, Patterdales, Border Terriers and Any Other Variety, all usually divided again into classes for dogs and bitches. Your terrier does not have to be registered with The Kennel Club or be a worker to compete, but it must be one of the breeds scheduled. Lurcher shows are run by the same organisation.

At these shows the makers of dog foods are most generous with prizes and there is often prize money as well. They are great days out for all country folk and for those who enjoy the outdoor life.

Matches

When it comes to judging for breed type, conformation and soundness, the most basic competition is the club match.

All dogs competing at a match must be over six months old and registered with The Kennel Club. No dog that has won a Challenge Certificate (CC) or Reserve Challenge Certificate (RCC) may compete in a match.

Most, if not all, canine societies run a series of matches throughout the year, and these culminate in a great evening around Christmas when the Match Dog of the Year is judged. Here all the

Best in Match dogs of the year and the Best Puppies compete for the honours.

At matches each exhibitor is given a number. The numbers are placed in a hat, and two are drawn out. The two dogs bearing these numbers are are judged against each other and the winner goes on to the next round. Once the first round is completed, the winning numbers go back into the hat and are re-drawn two at a time and the new pairs are judged against each other. This goes on until the last two dogs compete against each other for Best In Match. The same happens in the puppy match, which always starts the evening. Puppies must be over six months and must not exceed twelve months.

Rosettes are awarded to the winners, and sometimes packets of dog food, dog shampoo and the like which have been donated by firms specialising in such things.

Some people with pedigree dogs never exhibit anywhere except at club matches and derive great pleasure from these and all other activities run by their club. They get the chance to help out with refreshments, prepare the hall and sell raffle tickets. The friendly atmosphere at such occasions makes for a good social evening as well.

Exemption Shows

The smallest dog shows held are exemption shows. These are licensed by The Kennel Club and can be organised by anyone who applies for a licence, for which a payment is required.

In these shows there can only be four classes for pedigree dogs and it is not necessary for the dogs to be registered. The shows are always held for charity and often take place as an ancillary to small agricultural shows, horse shows, village and garden fêtes and the like, or may be run on their own. They provide great fun and pleasure for owners of pedigree dogs with no papers, as they are the only Kennel Club shows in which an unregistered pedigree dog may compete.

No dogs who are champions or have won CCs or RCCs may be entered. The four classes for pedigrees are usually Puppy, Sporting, Non-sporting and Open. There are always four, and often five, placings in each class, and there is a Best in Show (BIS) and a Best Puppy award. After the pedigree classes are concluded there will be some 'fun' classes: for instance, *Best Condition*, *Best Mover*, *Waggiest Tail* or *Dog Most Like Its Owner*.

These are great days out, and success at one of these events can provide encouragement for the more faint-hearted owners to enter their dogs in larger shows. Exemption wins often provide the spur needed to go on to greater things and are at the base of exhibitors' success stories.

Limited Shows

Between the exemption and limited shows there were, until quite recently, sanction shows. These were 25-class events that allowed both dog and new exhibitor a chance to acquire further ring experience. However, The Kennel Club has now discontinued licences for these, so the next step is the limited show. Most canine societies and some breed clubs run at least one limited show during the year. At an all-breed limited show, some breeds will be scheduled, but most of the classes will be for Any Variety (any breed of dog) or Any Variety Not Separately Classified (any breed that does not have designated classes). No CC or RCC winners may enter. Limited Shows are useful stepping stones for the new exhibitor before he or she goes on to the next stage.

Open Shows

As its name suggests, the open show is open to all exhibitors and all dogs. The number of classes can range from 75 to more than 200 and will include a number of breed as well as variety classes.

Championship Shows

About 28 general championship shows are held each year, most of them in the summer months. They are open to all, and it is here that dogs compete for the Challenge Certificates (CCs) that count towards the title of champion. These shows will be benched (see further on) and the number of dogs attending over a period of two or three days may be anything from 8000 to 15,000.

Many newcomers to the show ring seek to start their show career at these prestigious events and swiftly become disillusioned when their dogs are overlooked in large classes. The well-known kennels

A line-up of Staffordshire Bull Terriers. While most breeds are shown in profile, the bull breeds are mostly shown facing the judge. Photo: Robert Smith

that consistently produce winners are constantly there with quality stock. Owners of dogs of lesser merit cannot hope to be successful. To compete on equal terms at this level the exhibitor must have a reasonable specimen of his or her chosen breed, which is why I advise people purchasing puppies with a view to exhibiting to buy from top breeders. Top breeders have their reputations to consider and do not want substandard stock bearing their names to be seen in the ring, so by buying from them you get a fairer deal and have a better chance at big events. Nevertheless, my own opinion is that newcomers would do well to find their feet at matches and smaller shows before entering the very competitive world of championship shows.

Three Counties *Championship Show*   Date   10-12 June 1997

Breed _____   Sex _____

Kennel Club
Challenge Certificate

I am clearly of the opinion that

_____
(Name of Exhibit)

owned by _____
(Name of Owner)

is of such outstanding merit as to be worthy of the title of Champion.

(Signed)

_____
(Judge)

The coveted Challenge Certificate (CC).

Crufts Dog Show

This four-day championship dog show, held each March at the National Exhibition Centre in Birmingham, is owned and run by The Kennel Club. To enter Crufts, all dogs must have qualified; that is, they must have won a stated prize in a designated class at one of the other general championship or group or breed championship shows held in

15

the previous year. Others eligible for entry are:

- Dogs that have won at Crufts the previous year
- Dogs that have won a five-point Green Star of higher under the rules of the Irish Kennel Club.
- All champions, show champions, field or working trial champions or dogs that have qualified for Crufts dog and bitch obedience championship competition.
- All dogs entered in or who qualified for entry in The Kennel Club *Stud Book* in the previous year.

Even more coveted –
the Best of Breed (BOB) card.

The qualification for Crufts is published in the dog press each year, as well as in the schedules for the show.

At one time, Crufts was open to all exhibitors, but the escalating number of entries caused the show officials to bring in a qualification, as no venue would be large enough to contain all would-be entrants.

Group Shows

The breeds are divided into seven groups: Gundog, Working, Pastoral, Hound, Terrier, Utility and Toy. A list of the breeds eligible for each group will be found at the end of this book.

Group shows may be limited, open or championship events and are run by a club or clubs concerned with the breeds involved. They may be either benched or unbenched.

Breed Shows

These shows are run by a club concerned with the breed in question and are confined to that breed. They may be limited, open or championship, and benched or unbenched.

The Dog Press

To find out what shows are to be held in the future and check shows in your area, take out a subscription to one or both of the weekly dog papers: *Dog World* or *Our Dogs*.

These papers are essential to would-be exhibitors for, as well as giving information about forthcoming events, they have many pages of notes devoted to the various breeds, show reports and useful and interesting articles by canine writers.

Unbenched Shows

All the small shows are *unbenched*: in other words, there is no provision for the dogs as regards places where they can be tied up or confined.

In late autumn, winter and early spring the problem of what to do with the dog between classes is solved, as it can be left in the car with the windows slightly ajar. However, as soon as the weather becomes at all warm, dogs must not be left in cars. Many people these day invest in a wire cage of some sort or a large travelling box of lightweight plastic with a wire door. These can be taken to shows and placed in a corner or against the wall of the hall, and the dog can safely be shut in when it is not in the ring. Otherwise, the dog must be kept with the exhibitor.

When walking about the show with your dog on a lead or standing by a ringside, do keep the lead tight; do not allow your dog to sniff other dogs, or strange dogs to approach yours. All dogs should be under their owners' strict control.

While sitting at the ringside with your dog, particularly if it is large, do see that it does not lie in the ring. An exhibitor could trip over it. In any case, the rules state that no dog who is not entered in a class may be in the ring – even if it's asleep!

Benched Shows

Benching is found at the larger shows of over so many classes or when a certain number of dogs are entered. It will be found at most of the group shows and breed shows for the numerically superior breeds. All major championship shows are *benched*.

Benching is supplied by regular benching contractors and the size of the benches for each breed of dog is laid down by The Kennel Club. The benching is made of wooden trestles with metal backs and partitions, with wire racks above. Each bench is fitted with a ring at floor level at the back of the bench.

At some championship shows benching for toy dogs takes the form of cages, but exhibitors of toy and other smaller breeds, including many of the smaller terriers, prefer to bring cages and fit those on the benches to hold their dogs. However, any dog bigger than a Fox Terrier should wear a well-fitting collar, and to this is clipped one end of the bench chain. The other end of the chain slots through the ring provided and fastens to itself by means of a second clip. Great care should be taken that the chain is not left too long, thus enabling the dog to jump off the bench and get hung up, or too short, so that the dog can choke. No dog that is benched in this way should be left alone for more than 15 minutes without someone checking that it is safe and comfortable. Dogs should not be tied to the ring by leads, as these can be chewed through, allowing the dog to escape.

Above the bench you will find slotted in the wire mesh a card bearing your dog's number, and there is room to display any prize cards won. No advertising, apart from a card with the kennel name and address, is permitted over the bench.

Bags, boxes and coats can be stowed neatly under the bench. Remember that all benched shows are open to the public, who pay to view the dogs, so please do not fill your bench with belongings or hang towels over the front of the cage if you have benched your dog in this fashion; this is against Kennel Club rules.

Dogs are required to be on their benches during the day, except when being exercised or in the ring.

When To Leave

At most shows these days exhibitors may leave the show when their classes are over. However, if you wish to learn more about dogs and your breed in particular, it is a good idea to stay as long as you can and take an interest in the proceedings.

At large agricultural shows with a championship dog show as one of the attractions for the general public, exhibitors will be expected to stay until a given time; if you do not wish to abide by this rule it is as well not to enter. The stewards on the gates are instructed when to allow dogs out, but often much aggravation is caused by exhibitors who intend to leave when it suits them and not to abide by the rules.

Cleaning Up

At all shows there will be large notices urging you to clean up after your dog. Many valuable and irreplaceable venues have been lost to dog shows by the thoughtless behaviour of exhibitors who allow their dogs to foul and then walk on and leave the mess for others to walk in.

Carry a supply of plastic bags and, if your dog makes a mess, slip your hand into a bag, pick up the mess, turn the bag inside out and deposit it in one of the bins provided. Otherwise, all shows have a supply of shovels and buckets for use in such cases.

Every dog show is required to allot a space for exercising the dogs so that they can relieve themselves. Find out where this is as soon as you arrive at the show, and encourage your dog to use it. Car parks used by exhibitors and paths and roads leading into the venue should also be kept clean, as well as the venue itself, and it is up to

Please encourage your dog to relieve itself in the designated exercise area, and clean up after it.
Photo: Robert Smith

exhibitors to see that this is done; otherwise their enjoyable show days may be numbered. The anti-dog lobby is very active, as are the health and safety people, and any transgressions by the dog-owning public are likely to be penalised. Exhibitors of show dogs should set a good example.

Benching

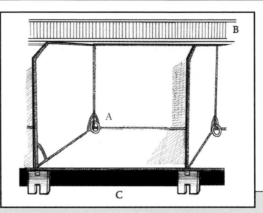

1 Benching.
A **Ring to which bench chain should be clipped.**
B **Rack holds card stating dog's number and any prize cards won.**
C **Space to stack bags**

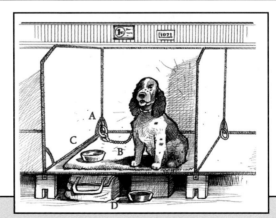

2 Dog correctly benched.
A **Bench chain with clip at each end.**
B **Rug.**
C **Water or food bowl. Bowl should not be left on bench with dog, but offered when required.**
D **Bags neatly stacked, not obscuring view of dog.**

3   The benching area. Here, one dog is secured to its bench by a collar and lead and one is in a carrying cage.

Photo: Robert Smith

Avoiding Disappointment

The Correct Show Type

Friends may tell you that your pedigree dog is beautiful and would surely win a prize in a show, but they may not necessarily be right! Unless they are engaged in breeding and showing dogs, preferably dogs of the same breed as your own, they are unlikely to know whether your dog is a show specimen.

When sitting with my dogs on the benches over the years, I have often been spoken to by people who admired the dogs and made such remarks as, 'My friend has one just like that!' or 'My Grannie had one just as beautiful!' Often, when you probe further, you find that the friend's or Grannie's dog was not even of the same breed.

Before setting out to show your dog, take the advice in the previous chapter and attend a show or two on your own. Do not hesitate to ask someone at the show who has the same breed for information. One thing doggy people love to do is to talk about their dogs, so you will soon have plenty of advice. However, you may find some of the advice conflicting; sift it all in your mind when you get home.

Entering your dog at an exemption show may help you to decide if it is worth pursuing the goals of open and championship show competition. At many exemption shows, particularly ones for the popular charities, you will find that the judge is someone well known in the dog world who is glad to come and judge, thus boosting the entry and ensuring that plenty of money is raised for the cause. These judges are always willing to respond to questions asked politely after the judging is completed, and the opinion of knowledgeable people is worth having. At some exemption shows the judges will be just starting on a judging career and may not know much about your breed. Even so, they should be able to tell you if the construction and movement are sound.

It is only by attending dog shows and visiting kennels that you can hope to learn enough about the breed to determine whether your

Miniature Dachshunds are weighed in the ring before they are shown. If you have one, do get it used to this at home. Photo: Sharkey

dog is a potential winner or just a loving friend who may bring a few rosettes and a lot of fun at exemption shows.

Training

A badly behaved dog has little chance of being placed. Judges have to be able to handle the dog in the ring: to lift its lips to check that the tooth formation is correct, to check the male for entirety and to feel the body, shoulders and head. If the dog has never been subjected to such an examination by a stranger it may object, pull away, be wild or even take fright.

A puppy bought with the idea of showing it in the future should be trained right from early puppyhood. A pup should begin to know how to behave from a very young age and, if it is brought up like that and the lessons are kindly, you will not end up with a 'teenage tearaway' of nine months whom the judge cannot examine and you find difficult to control. All young things need to learn that they must behave in a civilised manner and that they will be loved even more if they do.

23

Standing to be Handled

Dogs that are to be shown should be trained to stand and be handled. If you intend to start a career with a dog of, say, over a year old, then training must start at once and may take a few months. The dog must trot quietly beside you and not pull back, forth or to the side but maintain a steady and correct pace for the breed.

Get your family and friends to help you get your potential show dog used to standing still and being examined. Do not give lots of titbits during training, as this will make the dog look out for these instead of concentrating. A reward should only be given at the end of the lesson, after the last pat and a hearty 'Good Boy!' (or 'Good Girl!')

Training the puppy can start with setting it in the proper position when daily grooming takes place. Always make your puppy stand still while you lift the lips to see its teeth. As it gets older, show practice should be a short daily routine, and all friends coming in should be asked to go over the pup, if only to lift the lips and feel the body. The puppy who is so trained never objects to the judge going over it, as there is nothing new or frightening in the operation.

Lead Training

No puppy should start lead training until it is naturally balanced. Most puppies do not balance themselves correctly until about four months old. This is obvious if you watch them at play. They cut corners and fall over, often lose their footing and sit down hurriedly, or turn in a circle and tumble over. None of this harms them; it is simply part of the growing-up period. If you try to train a puppy before it is naturally balanced the little thing will be struggling to keep itself up on its legs.

Puppies who have been put on the lead too early often end up as poor movers, having been pulled out of shape, and once movement has been ruined there is no correcting it. For this reason, let the puppy destined for the show ring have free play and exercise coupled with an hour or so rest two or three times a day. It will grow better, stronger and mentally better adjusted if such a routine is followed. Regular meals are also a 'must', as is a ready supply of clean, cold water to drink.

I am not in favour of giving a lot of bribes in the shape of food to get dogs to obey. If they are shown the right way in easy steps and encouraged with kind words and patting, puppies will work out for themselves what is required and realise that a reward is forthcoming at the end of the lesson.

When the puppy looks sound on its legs it is time to start lead training.

Everyone has his own way of training a puppy to work quietly on a lead. The basics are to get the puppy used to wearing a collar before you start clipping a lead on. It is useful, once the lead is on, to accustom the puppy to being tied up. It may object at first, but staying with it and talking to it will calm the initial reaction. When the puppy is used to being tied up for a few minutes each day for four or five days it will accept that it cannot get away, and settle down. A puppy who quietly accepts being tied up will usually quietly accept the lead when walking as well. Also, the fact that pups trained in this way are no problem to tie up will be invaluable at benched shows.

Once it is on the lead, the cardinal rule is never to let the puppy get away from you by slipping its collar, biting through the lead or by the lead slipping through your hands. If any of these happen once, you have to start all over again to convince the pup that it has not won and you are still the boss.

When the puppy is trotting happily beside you, you can start to take it on regular walks. Make sure that the distance is not too long; it must be tailored to the size and requirements of the breed, and hints on this can be found in the relevant breed books.

Once the puppy is walking well and going out regularly, do take some of the walks in areas where the pup can see people, vehicles and other dogs so that it is well socialised before stepping into the spotlight of the showring. I used to take mine to a busy car park and walk them about among the cars and people.

Ring Training

Once your dog is used to regular walks you can start on ring training. If you have friends with dogs, ask them and their dogs to tea, set up a mini-ring and all of you walk around in a circle leading the dogs. If your dog gets used to this it will not be alarmed when it enters the ring at its first show. You can also practise standing your dog, letting your friends act as the judge and examine it, and then trot your dog around to let them see its movement.

A visit to a junk shop should provide you with a couple of large mirrors quite cheaply. Place them one each end of the path or either side of the lawn and trot the dog between them. You can then assess the movement and correct what you think is wrong. It is also helpful to pose, or *stack*, the dog in front of one of the mirrors so that you can see what you are doing wrong and correct it if necessary.

Ringcraft Classes

Most canine societies now hold ringcraft sessions, but these are only as useful as the person taking the lesson. To take a young puppy to a ring training class without some preparation may put it off for life.

One hazard at ringcraft evenings is the people who bring adult dogs who are very much out of control. It can be frightening for the young puppy to be lunged at or pursued around the ring by an untrained and possibly untrainable dog. Dogs who are wild in the ring cannot be examined and therefore have no chance of being placed in the winning line-up. It is up to you to present your dog as a well behaved, amiable character whom the judge is delighted to examine.

Show Temperament

A word of warning: should your dog of whatever age show any signs of poor temperament, do not enter it for shows. Dogs that growl are usually side-lined or sent from the ring; dogs that bite or attempt to bite may be reported to The Kennel Club, and the owners will have to account for their dogs' actions. If your dog has a temperament problem – leave it at home. The same can be said of very nervous dogs, who are also potentially dangerous dogs. Dogs have only two methods of defence when frightened: to turn and bolt (which they cannot do if on a lead) or to bite. A nervous dog is therefore an anxiety in the ring and very unlikely to grow out of it sufficiently to make a successful show dog.

This Welsh Springer Spaniel's handler is standing well back from his dog and maintaining finger-tip control to make the dog look its best. Photo: Robert Smith

Baiting

Do not feed or *bait* your dog in the ring. As I have said before, it is far better to train the dog to expect the titbit *after* it has performed the required actions. If you take a few pieces of biscuit in your pocket, only give the dog one after it has been seen and moved by the judge, and not again until you are both out of the ring.

Dogs who are continually fed in the ring often have their chances spoilt, as the judge finds it impossible to examine the dog's head and, should they be able to see the teeth, often find them covered in biscuit or liver. The more a dog is fed in the ring, the wilder it becomes. It is also unfair to the others if you take food into the ring, because if it gets left where your dog has been standing it may distract the dog who has been properly trained.

A dog who misbehaves in the ring or constantly has to be fed may lose a place or even the chance of being pulled out in the line-up if all other things are equal. It is a great disappointment to the owner when such a thing occurs.

27

Behaviour in the Ring

1 **Feeding titbits in the ring can make the dog wild or badly behaved.**

2 Exhibitors need to use both hands to steady their dogs should a judge approach from the front. Most dogs lean backwards if approached this way.

3 Dogs that have been properly trained stand without bribes. They know they will be rewarded when they leave the ring.

Hounds show best free standing, like this Beagle. They must be trained to do this at home. Photo: Robert Smith

Again, you should not take a ball or squeaky toy into the ring. By doing this you risk distracting other people's dogs.

Free Standing

Try to train your dog to free stand (that is, to go into the correct pose without being manipulated by the handler). It will really look much more impressive than if you have to go down on your knees and hold it in position. Free standing dogs are naturally balanced and present a better outline. Training for this method can be carried out at home by teaching the dog to stand alone at the end of the lead, alert and waiting for something in your pocket that it knows will be its reward for correct behaviour. Do not give the reward until the exercise is complete; in the ring, do not give the reward until the judge has moved on to the next dog. This kind of training takes longer and requires great patience, but can be very satisfactory.

Over Showing

A word of warning: dogs can be over shown. However enthusiastic you become for showing dogs, and this is likely to happen if your dog

Although posed on the table for the judge's examination, most Toys are show-offs and show free standing at ground level, like this Chihuahua. Photo: Robert Smith

is successful at its first show, do limit the number of shows you enter. A long day at a show, plus all the travelling, is very tiring for a dog

Ch Johnstounburn Gold Trim of Yadnum, owned by Miss Vera Munday. Yorkshire Terriers are the only breed to be shown off the ground. Their owners pose them in the ring on travelling boxes covered in red or blue velvet. Photo: Robert Smith

and more so for a puppy. Dogs can get bored with shows, and then they do not give of their best, or even pack up showing altogether. Ration the number of shows you enter and, if you feel you simply must go to a show, go without the dog; such visits provide good opportunities to learn more about your breed and the world of showing.

31

Presentation

No matter how well your dog behaves it is unlikely to be successful unless correctly fed, conditioned and presented. The dog needs to have firm flesh and be well muscled, and these things can only be achieved by good feeding at regular times and sufficient exercise of the right kind. Remember: fat is not fit!

A beautifully groomed Scottish Terrier:
Mrs Maureen Micklethwaite's Ch Glenecker Gracie.
Photo: Anne Roslin-Williams

Grooming

Regular grooming ensures that skin and coat are in prime condition. Those who opt for a smooth-coated breed such as a Whippet or Smooth Fox Terrier will have to carry out only light trimming for a show, but it is even more important for such breeds to be sound and well muscled since they have no coat to cover up the faults.

For all breeds it is imperative that the feet are kept in good order by regular clipping of the nails; about every two weeks is a rough guide. Long nails cause the toes to splay out and the dog to move unevenly. Many people say they have trouble cutting their dogs' nails but, if a puppy is accustomed to this from the start, there should be no trouble. Never try to cut a puppy's nails with scissors. They are not sharp enough and pull the nail, causing it to hurt, and puppies have long memories. Use a proper nail clipper.

Ears should be cleaned with cotton wool.

Smooth-coated dogs come up well if groomed with a hound glove and finished off by polishing with a piece of silk.

All coated breeds need some form of trimming, and the correct

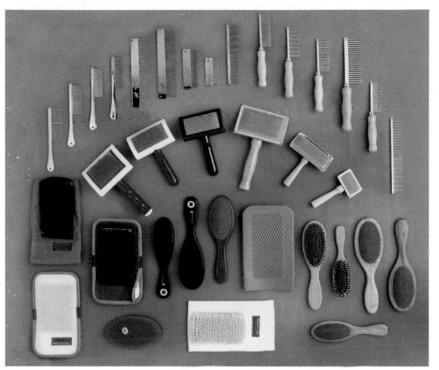

Grooming equipment: slickers, combs, brushes and hound gloves.

way to set about this is to ask an established exhibitor to show you how to do it. Most breed books have a chapter on show preparation and, with the tips from the exhibitor and constant reference to the book, in time you will be able to do the job satisfactorily. Do buy a book by a British exhibitor. American breed books give advice on grooming the American way, which is not applicable in this country. Do not despair if your first attempts look amateurish: only with practice will you learn how to do an expert job. Daily grooming is essential if coats are not to get out of hand, and this applies particularly to such breeds as Bichons, Pekingese and Poodles.

Many people take their first show dog of a coated breed to a grooming parlour to be prepared – and many have a rude shock when they collect their dogs. Not many parlours have staff qualified to prepare dogs for show, and to collect your Cocker Spaniel or Wire Fox Terrier and find it has been clipped all over can be devastating.

In every breed there are people who groom for show for other exhibitors, but there are fewer than in the past. For this reason, along with all the other things, new exhibitors need to know how to prepare their dogs' coats themselves.

To avoid disappointment, do not show your dog when it is out of coat. If it is a very good specimen it may be highly placed under some judges, but there are others who will not place an exhibit that is not in full coat. You may not find out into which category your judge falls until too late!

When Not To Show

It is unwise to show a dog who has had a wound stitched, a leg shaved for an injection or who has a bald patch. Competition in most breeds is so fierce these days that only dogs in first-class condition can go to the top. Similarly, never show your dog if it has gone lame. A lame dog cannot compete on equal terms with dogs that are sound. It is terribly disappointing to have to miss a show for which you have entered but, unless the dog is 100%, it is a waste of time and can prove very dispiriting.

There is no Kennel Club rule stating that bitches in season cannot compete but I consider it very unfair to take a bitch on heat to a show. At championship events the sexes are divided but, at all other shows, dogs and bitches compete together, so a bitch on heat can distract all the male dogs in her class and, by leaving her scent in the ring, disrupt males in succeeding classes. Anyway, a bitch in season never gives of her best and, if she is light in colour, she will have stained 'trousers'. I have never shown a bitch in season. There will be plenty more shows, and other exhibitors will be grateful that you have put them above your own ambitions. It is unwise to take a bitch in whelp to a show as this could cause exhaustion and distress.

Everything you need for your dog can be bought on the stands at championship shows.

Do not take your dog to the show if it evinces any sign of illness in the days immediately before the show or on the show day itself. When you enter the show you sign an undertaking not to take a sick dog to the event so, if

A superbly presented Cocker Spaniel: Mr Armstrong's Sh Ch Britcon Troubador.

you do and it has to have veterinary treatment at the show, you may find yourself in trouble. Apart from that, it is grossly unfair to take a dog on a journey for a long day at a show when it is feeling unwell.

One of the most usual infectious ailments is kennel cough. It can spread rapidly so, if your dog is coughing, leave it at home.

Dealing With Travel Sickness

Among the hazards of conveying dogs to shows are dribbling and travel sickness. Some dogs do not travel well and, even if they only slobber all the way, they can get themselves into a mess.

Numerous preparations are available to treat dogs with this distressing complaint, and you may find one that relieves your dog of its trouble. If you have a poor traveller, these tips could be useful:

- Do not feed your dog immediately before your journey.
- Try to place it in a crate in the front of the car or on the back seat rather than behind the rear grill in an estate car. Of course, if it is a big dog, you will have little option but to leave it in the back.
- Stop several times on the way to let the dog walk around and relieve itself. Sponge its mouth with water but do not let it drink.
- A large towel tied around the dog can collect excess dribble.

Start early for the show so that you have plenty of time to do a clean-up job when you arrive at the show, well before your classes. Give your dog a drink and a little dry food as soon as it is perky again. This will be quite soon; dogs recover quickly once on *terra firma*!

Last Minute Grooming at the Show

All your serious grooming and trimming should have been done at home so that you have a minimum of work to do at the show. However, for heavy-coated dogs, grooming goes on most of the time before a class. Please take a plastic bag with you and clear up all your clippings and combings, and do leave the area where you have been in a clean condition.

The Well-Groomed Exhibitor

Not only should your dog be presented in pristine order; it helps if you too are neat and tidy. In the past, people were always well turned out in the rings, and it is only since casual wear became acceptable for almost every occasion that exhibitors have become sloppily dressed. If you have a nice dog over whose preparation you have slaved for days, doesn't it make sense to dress smartly so that the dog has a nice background to be seen against? It does not take much effort to pack a skirt or trousers and jacket to put on before you show the dog. To come dressed for the ring with a large apron or overall to put on while you prepare the dog is even less effort.

Dirty, torn jeans, scuffed trainers, ill-fitting T-shirts, jogging suits, shell suits and shorts have all been seen many times in the ring. They do nothing for the exhibitor or the exhibit. At most shows, ringsiders are busy with their video cameras. You might just have a shock to see yourself on one of their films at a future doggy gathering – or, far worse, if local television reporters attend the show and you are shown in all your grunge to the viewing public.

Scruffy exhibitors do not give a very good image of those connected with the world of dogs. Those cleanly and neatly dressed signal that they have expectations; those who take no trouble are really signalling that they do not think they have much of a chance of seeing their dogs placed.

Think carefully about colour when you are choosing your outfit. Do not wear black skirt or trousers when showing a black or black-and-white dog, as it (or portions of it) will then disappear into the background. Similarly, do not wear brown when showing a liver dog or russet when showing a tan or tan-and-white. Choose a contrasting colour: red and green are good choices for black dogs, biscuit or green for brown, blue for white and so on. Put yourself in the place of the judge and consider what he or she will observe when you stand your dog. Will the dog be thrown into sharp relief or swallowed up into the unfortunate background you've created?

Shows now have to provide grooming areas where cages and tables can be left.

Sensible, low-heeled shoes are the best choice for women exhibitors. Some come in high heels and remove their shoes before moving the dog. Apart from the danger – after all, you don't know what is lying about in the ring – feet, bare or stockinged, are hardly an edifying sight for the judge, the other exhibitors or the ringside!

Women whose skirts are too short or too tight can come unstuck. As they bend and stretch to show off their dogs, they often inadvertently show off more of themselves than they intend.

Ladies with long manes of hair are advised to pin it up or tie it back before entering the ring. If they bend attentively over their dogs, the hair falls forward and the dog is masked from the judge.

Male exhibitors, particularly those of large build, should always wear shirts that tuck in well. The ringside has all too often been treated to off-putting sightings of bare flesh as polo or T-shirts ride up and trousers ride down.

Remember that you, as much as your dog, are on show. The ringside can be very cruel if, by your bizarre appearance, you give them cause.

How Not to Dress

1 **Do wear a comfortable pair of shoes. Removing footwear is unnecessary and you may step in something, which, besides being unpleasant for you and the ringside, would spoil your concentration.**

2 **Exhibitors should remember that their backs are to most of the spectators, and dress accordingly. Gentlemen should tuck their shirts in!**

3 This Irish Red and White Setter's handler has
the dog well positioned and her hands nicely
placed but her loose white blouse confuses the
outline. A contrasting colour like green and a
closer fit would be better.

Photo: Robert Smith

Costs

Anyone venturing into the world of dog showing would be well advised to have a budget.

Obtaining a Show Dog

If you already own a pedigree dog suitable for show, your initial outlay has already been made. If your dog was originally bought at a reasonable price from a breeder who considered at the time that it was unlikely to make a show specimen, but subsequent events have proved otherwise, you are indeed one of the lucky ones! Geese can turn into swans, and it is not unknown for a pup bought purely as a pet from a good kennel to become quite a big winner.

If, however, you have no dog but wish to own one you can show successfully, go to a well-known and well-recommended breeder and buy from a well-bred litter. Most of the puppies, given the right rearing, treatment and average luck, should make good in the ring. For such a puppy you should expect to pay a good price.

The best and most responsible breeders do not churn out endless litters each year, but breed selectively and seldom, so you may have to wait a long time for a suitable puppy to become available. Do be patient – it will avail you nothing to rush off and buy the first puppy on offer. Far better to wait for a selectively-bred litter and have a puppy from this. Never buy a puppy from a pet shop (no reputable one would sell a puppy anyway) or a puppy farm. It is worth noting also that litters advertised in local papers are usually from pet bitches and seldom of show quality.

My advice is to attend shows and stay by the ring of your chosen breed, talking to people at the ringside and listening to what they have to say. You will soon learn which kennels produce stock that wins regularly at shows, not only for the breeder but also for those who have purchased stock from the kennel. At whatever show you attend, always buy a catalogue. This gives details of the dogs entered and their breeding and, by comparing these, you will get a good idea of which kennels to approach for a likely puppy.

On sale at the show: bowls of all shapes and sizes, wire cages and plastic kennels.
Photo: Robert Smith

When you go to good kennels to see litters you will also see the dam and possibly the sire. Often you will also see older dogs and bitches related to the litter, so you will get a good idea of the type bred and how a puppy is likely to turn out.

Initial Outlay

To ensure that you have enough money for your initial purchase and the first essentials I suggest you lay aside not less than £1000.

First you have the cost of the puppy, which will take up a large slice of this sum. The puppy may not be inoculated, so that will be your first expense, along with bed, bowls, grooming kit and so on.

Insurance

Today there are many canine insurance schemes. Your puppy may already be insured when you buy it but, if not, you may wish to take out cover. If you take out insurance just to cover veterinary bills you will probably find you are required to pay the first £25 or so of the claim and that inoculations, boosters and so on are not covered. The cheapest insurance is likely to set you back about £100 a year. (In fact, a puppy correctly fed and cared for should not need that amount of veterinary treatment in a year. If it does, it is unlikely to make a useful show specimen.)

It is also possible to insure against accidents, death and loss.

I suggest you procure brochures from various firms specialising in canine insurance and have them read (especially the small print) by someone wise in the ways of insurance before deciding.

Food Bills

Food bills can be large or small, depending on how you choose to feed your dog. With so many dog foods on the market and the heavy advertising, new owners get confused. Ask the breeder of your dog for advice on feeding it.

Grooming Equipment

Equipment for grooming and exercising will be needed as the puppy grows. If you have chosen a coated breed a proper grooming table is a good investment. The correct brushes and grooming tools for your breed should be purchased from a good firm. The best work out the cheapest in the long run, perform to a high standard and last longest. If you have a breed on which electric clippers are used for show preparation you will need these once the dog is grown up, but do not try to use them without being given some instruction.

Travelling Equipment

A wire crate or plastic travelling box with a wire front will be be found most useful, especially for travelling and confining dogs at unbenched shows. If you have chosen one of the larger breeds your car will need to be fitted with a dog guard or fitted wire compartment. Again, choose the best quality, which will be the strongest and most durable. The dog can then be carried in the rear of the vehicle and will be prevented from jumping forward if excited and perhaps causing an accident. For safety's sake, all dogs should either be secured in this way or carried in a crate or box.

Latest on the market: a cage on wheels. This Pug is enjoying a trouble-free ride.
Photo: Robert Smith

Be Attentive in the Ring

1 These exhibitors are totally inattentive and are
allowing their dogs to sniff the ground. It is
difficult to get the attention of dogs immediately if
they have picked up a good scent.

2 This Welsh Springer Spaniel is walking along
attentively, its head held high, but the slip lead is
too tight for my taste. Photo: Robert Smith

3 This exhibitor is handling her Bichon Frisé attentively, according to the judge's instructions.

4 These two exhibitors are so busy gossiping that they have not realised that the judge is trying to get their attention.

Arriving by coach. Many long-distance exhibitors charter coaches to take them to the show. Photo: Robert Smith

Subscriptions and Show Expenses

Subscriptions to canine and breed societies, together with the cost of the weekly dog papers, must come into the equation, and another expense will be the cost of entry to shows.

Entry fees vary according to the type and size of the show. At the time of writing, the cost at exemption shows is approximately £1 a class and limit shows charge roughly £2 and open shows £3–£5. Most general championship shows range from £10–£17 a class; second entries, that is for the same dog entered in one or two further classes, are £1–£2. Crufts entry fees are £18 per class. Breed clubs have a varying scale of charges: anything from perhaps £5 a class upwards, according to the finances of the club, the level of support and the size and scope of the show. Expect the cost of entries to rise in the coming years. Catalogues can be £2–£6 but are a necessary part of showing and should be kept carefully for reference.

On top of this, larger shows often have a charge for parking. Add to all this your travelling expenses and food for the day. Should the show fall on a week day and you have a job or family, a day's pay lost or the cost of a sitter for the children or elderly dependants should be included.

You will find once you start showing regularly that your biggest expense is travelling. Petrol, oil, tyres and wear and tear on the car must come into the equation. Regular servicing and repairs must be carried out if you are to avoid the drama of breakdown on the way to the show. Subscription to the AA or RAC is very necessary, and all exhibitors should carry a mobile telephone now that these are so cheap and readily available.

In many areas, such as Scotland, Wales, the North of England and the far South West, coaches are organised to transport exhibitors and their dogs to shows that are far from their base. These are much cheaper and easier than taking a car, and a lively and amusing way to travel.

Most exhibitors say quite cheerfully that they never count the cost – if they did they might be frightened into giving up! In any case, whatever hobby you choose to pursue is going to cost you money, and showing dogs is no more expensive, and sometimes less so, than various other outdoor leisure activities.

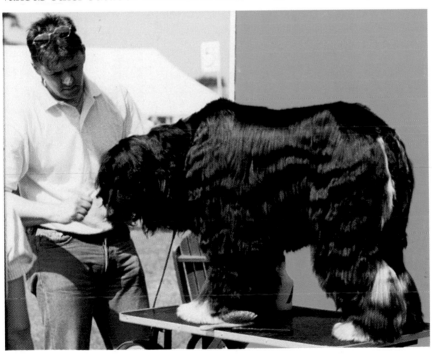

Heavily coated breeds need constant grooming and the correct equipment for the breed must be bought.

Showing and the Family

However enthusiastic you are about entering the world of dog shows, your family may not be quite so enthusiastic about the idea. If you live alone you have only yourself to please. Even so, if you have more than one dog it is wise to take into account that the dogs not going to the show will need to be looked after for the day. This will involve relying on friends, engaging a sitter or placing the dogs in kennels.

Showing and Other Family Members

Those living with parents may find that either or both parents enter into the new plans with enthusiasm – that is, as long as they like dogs and realise that showing dogs *does* upset the ordered routine.

If you are married you may find your husband or wife less than enthusiastic. I speak from experience. When I was first married I hoped that my husband would be as excited about showing as I was. Not so – one show, and he vowed he would never go to another. It was years before he finally consented to accompany me, and then only because I was judging. I don't think he ever again went to a show where I was exhibiting. However, he liked the dogs and was very cooperative about attending to those I left at home.

It's a sign of the times that today more and more dogs are entered in joint names of husband and wife or partners, both of whom attend the show and are equally enthusiastic about the show world.

Allergic Reactions

If you have children, especially small ones, and are buying a dog or puppy for show, be very sure that the children are not likely to suffer asthma attacks as a result of dog hair. So many people have had their hopes dashed when, after buying a puppy and becoming fond of it, they find that some member of the family is allergic to hair and the dog has to go. However, there are non-shedding breeds such as Poodles and Bichons that asthmatics can keep with no ill effects. I knew one lady, a chronic asthmatic, who lived happily with three

Poodles, but she could not go into a house where there was a shedding breed. If you have an asthmatic family member, then, a non-shedding breed might be the answer, although the family member in question would not be able to go to shows.

Children at Shows

Then there is the care of small children on show days. Many people now bring their families, some with tiny babies in prams or carrycots. Dog shows are really not the best places for small children; they are dirty and draughty and go on for a long time. The children become bored and fretful, and it is impossible to concentrate on doing a good job in the ring if you are worried when the baby cries or concerned about what your little dears are getting up to at the ringside. Many people bring toys to amuse small children, and I have actually seen toy cars hurtling across the ring during judging, propelled by small persons who see that lovely expanse of floor as a fantastic race track.

Many children of school age are as interested in showing as their parents and eagerly take part in preparing the dogs and compete in children's handling competitions. Many are members of The Kennel Club Junior Organisation and so have plenty to occupy their time. But some children brought to the shows, often young boys, are bored to death with the whole thing and get up to mischief, even doing a considerable amount of damage. Children have been seen on the tops of marquees, sliding from top to bottom. Apart from the obvious danger, such behaviour can result in very costly damage. At one show, vandalism by youngsters necessitated the expenditure of several thousands of pounds on rebuilding the permanent lavatories. At another, two young boys got into a store, started a machine and caused £2000 worth of damage. Most show schedules nowadays have a notice that urges parents to keep their children under control and some state that any damage done by children must be paid for by parents.

If you are showing dogs you simply cannot keep your eyes on bored, active children, so it is far better to leave children who are not interested in showing with friends or relations. I do realise that it is not always possible to farm children out for the day; sometimes they simply have to accompany you. In this case, I do urge you to bring an adult friend who is willing to take charge of the children while you are engaged in preparing and showing the dog.

Children must not be allowed to run up and down the benches, disturbing the dogs and annoying other exhibitors. Children with no fear of dogs must be taught that it is unwise to go up to a strange dog without the owner's permission and that being cheeky to other exhibitors is not to be tolerated.

Arrangements for the Disabled

Arrangements for the disabled, both exhibitors and interested visitors to dog shows, are much better now than in former days. Most shows, if not all, have special car parks for cars bearing orange stickers. At the big championship shows cars are allowed to stop at the doors to allow disabled visitors to alight or buses with wheelchair ramps are laid on from the car park to the hall. All halls now have toilet facilities for disabled people and most large halls have ramps as well as steps. A number of exhibitors now show their dogs from wheelchairs and I have not seen the other dogs in a ring where there is a wheelchair be at all disconcerted.

One satisfactory aspect of modern showing is that all are made welcome and there are proper facilities for the less able.

Taking Photographs

It is understandable that you would like to record the exploits of your dog when it enters the show ring. If you have a companion with you who is wielding a camcorder, do please see that people at the ringside are not inconvenienced. If an ordinary camera is being used, remember that you are not allowed in the ring to take photographs: these must be taken outside the ring, after the judging. If you take photographs from the ringside, do not use a flash, as this disturbs the dogs and you will earn a rebuke from the steward.

First Aid Provision

Should you or any of your companions be taken ill at a show, all societies have worked out emergency plans that swiftly go into operation. Every large show has a doctor present on the show ground and at smaller shows doctors are on call. Most shows also have Red

Many children from dog-showing families become members of the KCJO.
Model: Tamara Dawson

Cross or St John's Ambulance cover, complete with ambulance, so first aid or a trip to the hospital can easily be arranged.

Sick dogs too are provided for. A veterinary surgeon is present at each big show and a special room or tent is set aside for sick or injured dogs. At small shows vets are always on call.

Facilities for Unentered Dogs

You may not take unentered dogs into shows so, if you have a pet dog as well as a show dog, leave it at home or with a friend.

Small shows have no facilities for housing unentered dogs. Some big shows have a tent outside the gates where unentered dogs may be left in crates or cages. Some such tents have a small amount of benching. These facilities are often provided by a dogs' home or similar charity, so it is usual to make a donation to the organisation concerned for the service it provides.

Do not bring unentered dogs and leave them all day in your car. Cars soon heat up even in quite mild weather, and dogs can suffer great distress and even die if the car gets too hot. Windows may be smashed to release dogs that seem to be in distressed and you cannot be traced on the show ground, and you risk having your entries returned for future shows of that society and being prosecuted for cruelty by the RSPCA.

Seating

Not all shows have a great deal of seating at the ringside. For this reason, if you are accompanied by older friends or relatives, it is wise to bring folding chairs so that they can watch the judging in comfort.

Picnics and Litter

If you bring a picnic, do not eat it at the ringside. Food is a great temptation even to the best trained dog, and those in the ring are very distracted by rustling crisp bags or the sight of people unwrapping and gnawing sandwiches. Find a spot away from the ring for your meal.

If you bring cups or glasses from the bar to your picnic spot, please return them. Smashed china and glass have caused cut feet in both dogs and humans.

Please take all your litter home or place it in the bins or bags provided; don't chuck it on the floor or under your bench. At small shows the committee have to leave the hall spotless, and it seems unfair that they should have to spend an hour or so clearing up after exhibitors and ringsiders who could quite easily clear up after themselves. Committee members work in an honorary capacity and, although they expect to ply the broom when everyone has left, they should not be expected to clear up dogs' hair clippings, plastic cups and bottles, drink cans or paper bags.

An interest in showing dogs often begins at a very early age.
Photo: Robert Smith

Final plea to those who smoke or chew gum: please do not grind your cigarette stubs or your gum under your heel in the hall. Both take hours to clean off and sometimes the floor is permanently marked, so your thoughtlessness could mean the loss of the venue for future shows.

Moving for the Judge

When asked to move your dog in a straight line down the ring and back, try not to come off course. If there is a mat, keep the dog on it. Do not carry food or the dog will bend towards you and so be unable to move straight.

1 The lead should be slightly slack, but you should be in contact with the dog at all times. Keep the dog straight and a little away from you.

2 Turn neatly at the end of the ring without changing pace and bring the dog directly to the judge. Stop a metre or so from the judge and allow the dog to stand naturally.

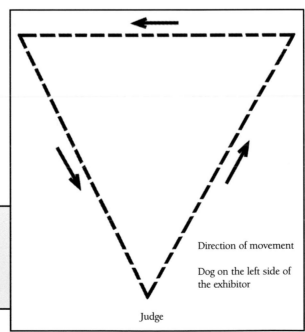

The correct way to walk a triangle when so requested.

Direction of movement

Dog on the left side of the exhibitor

Judge

Filling In the Forms

No occupation, business or even hobby can be enjoyed today without a great deal of tedious form filling, and dog showing is no exception.

Transfer of Ownership

Your prospective show dog will have come to you complete with registration certificate. All litters have to be registered by the breeder, so the first thing you must do is transfer the dog to your name. On the back of the registration certificate you will find the space in which you, as the new owner, fill in your name and address and other relevant details required. Do read all the instructions carefully and use block capitals for all the wording except your signature. If the dog is to be registered in joint names then both names must be entered and both parties must sign the form. The form is then sent to The Kennel Club with the appropriate fee. In a week or so you will receive the transfer certificate, which means that the dog is officially in your ownership.

Show Entry Forms

Shows are advertised in the dog press and a schedule can be obtained by contacting the show secretary. When this arrives, look to see if your breed is *classified* (has classes dedicated to it). In the schedule you will find a *Definition of Classes*, which clarifies the ages at which exhibits qualify for the Puppy, Junior, Yearling and Veteran classes and the rules for entry in other classes.

Entering a dog for any show other than exemption entails filling in an entry form. Entry forms arrive with the schedule and can be large or small, depending on the size and importance of the show.

On the entry form you will find the name and address of the secretary to whom the completed form must be sent and the date of 'entries closing'. This means that all entries must be received before the date stated.

All entry forms contain a declaration printed above the space for the signature and, in signing the form, you agree to abide by this declaration. Firstly, you declare that you will abide by the rules and regulations of The Kennel Club; secondly, that you will not knowingly bring a dog that has been exposed to an infectious or contagious disease to the show; thirdly, that the dog is prepared for exhibition in accordance with the rules; and finally that, to your knowledge, the dog has not suffered any disqualification.

A typical entry form for a championship show.

Entry forms are fairly self-explanatory, but it is amazing what a muddle some exhibitors get into when completing them. Although block capitals are required, many people still write the details in longhand. This leads to wrong information being printed in the catalogue when the printers cannot decipher the handwriting. Do use block capitals for all wording except your signature.

The first space on the form is for the name(s) of the dog(s) to be entered, but these must all be of the same breed. Should you wish to enter two dogs of different breeds, two separate entry forms must be completed. The details required are the *name* of each dog, its *breed*, *sex*, *date of birth*, *breeder*, *sire*, *dam* and the numbers of the *classes* in which it it to be entered. To take these singly:

- *Name* Only the name shown on the dog's registration certificate should be entered: pet names are not required, although new exhibitors have been known to enter these as well.
- *Breed* If your dog belongs to a breed with several sizes, such as the Poodle, indicate which size (Toy Poodle, Miniature Poodle or Standard Poodle).
- *Sex* In this column it is usual to enter *D* or *B* for Dog or Bitch, although it is quite in order to enter *M* or *F* for Male or Female.
- *Date of Birth* This can be written either as *8 Sept 1994* or as *8/9/94*. The latter is neater.
- *Breeder* You will find the breeder's name on the registration document. You may not enter your dog in a class that its breeder is judging.
- *Sire/Dam* These spaces are for the registered sire (father) of the dog and its dam (mother). This information will be found on the pedigree as well as the registration certificate of your dog.
- *Classes* The next space is for the numbers of the classes in which you want to enter your dog. If you turn to the page for your breed in the schedule you will find a number against each class for your breed. The number, not the name of the class, should be entered. The schedule will perhaps read *142 Puppy* or, at some championship shows, just *142 PD* or *PB*. If you want to enter this class, just enter *142*. In an open show you will perhaps want to enter some of the variety classes. These are usually found at the end of the schedule, although for some smaller shows Any Variety Puppy classes are at the beginning. Enter the classes in which you want to show your dog in numerical order.

Having completed this part of the form correctly, fill in the bottom right-hand portion, which asks for the name(s) and address of the owner(s) – again, in *clear block capitals*, please. If the dog is owned in partnership, the names of both partners must be printed and both must sign the declaration.

Each entry form has a panel on the top right-hand side which gives the fees for the classes and, for larger shows, the cost of a prepaid catalogue and for car or caravan parking and states whether a disabled label is required. Once you have completed the form, all that remains is to write a cheque or buy a postal order to cover the costs and post it with your entry form to the secretary. Bigger shows often provide an addressed envelope with their schedules.

Do not wait until the last moment, such as the night before entries close, to post your entry. Many people do, and their entries arrive too late and are returned. Post at least three days before the closing date, always using a first-class stamp, and it is wise, especially for entries to championship shows, to ask your post office for a certificate of posting. This is in case your entry is lost in the post; if this happens, no wins at the show will be sanctioned unless you can supply authenticated proof of posting.

It is not wise to send cash with entries but, if your bank account is running low, please do not send a cheque that may not be honoured. This causes a great deal of work and expense for shows and secretaries, not to mention embarrassment and disappointment for the exhibitor, as the entry will not be accepted.

Keeping Records

It is essential to keep a show record for your dog. Either on disc or in a show record book, note down every show entered, with classes, judge and any wins. If your dog proves a good winner you will need this record, as you will have a full list of the number of first prizes it has won in which classes. This guards against any mistakes in entering future shows.

Criteria for Classes

Do check your dog's date of birth when entering classes for which age is a factor. These are as follows:

A class line of Dalmatians at a championship show. In the background, one of the tents where the dogs are benched. Photo: Robert Smith

- *Minor Puppy* Dogs entered must be six months and not exceeding nine months of age.
- *Puppy* Dogs entered must be six months and not exceeding twelve months of age.
- *Junior* Dogs entered must be six months and not exceeding eighteen months of age.
- *Yearling* Dogs over six months and up to two years of age.
- *Veteran* Definitions vary, but the dog usually has to be seven years or older. Some shows have a Veteran class for dogs of seven to ten years and a Vintage class for dogs of eleven years and older.

In all cases the dog's age must be taken up to the first day of the show. For instance, if the show is held on 8 September and your puppy was born on 8 March, it can go into Minor Puppy; if it was born on 9 March, it is one day too young to be entered.

Except for Open, entry criteria for all classes are geared to the number of first prizes the dog has won. For instance, in Post Graduate, the dog would be ineligible if it had won five or more first prizes (prizes won in puppy classes do not count) or if it had won a Challenge Certificate (CC). Each adult class has a similar proviso, so read the definitions of classes carefully before entering.

The correct way to present a Staffordshire Bull Terrier to the judge.
Photo: Robert Smith

Showing Dogs from the Table

1 **Wrong** **The dog objects to having his muzzle held, so leans back from handler. The hand on the shoulder blocks the outline.**

2 **Wrong Dog's tail is down, it is standing awkwardly and its handler is standing too close and leaning over. Dog's outline obscured by handler's tie and hand on the throat.**

3 **Wrong** Lead in wrong hand, so handler has no control over dog.

4 **Correct** Lead in correct hand with spare gathered up out of the way. Handler stands behind but nicely away from dog, using free hand to control hind-quarters and tail. The whole dog , in balance, can now be seen by the judge.

Photos: Sharkey
Model: the Parson Jack Russell Terrier Howlbeck Uno Who
with owner/breeder Mr G W Simpson

If you are entering for Crufts you will find a special box on the entry form in which to note the show, with date and class win, that qualifies your dog for entry. Crufts is the only show where a dog cannot be entered as of right, but must have won a placing in a designated class at a championship show in the 12 months prior to the show. A list of qualifying classes is printed in the Crufts schedules.

Junior Warrant

A Junior Warrant is awarded to a dog who has accumulated 24 points in breed classes between the ages of 6 and 18 months. One point is awarded for each first prize won in a breed class at an open show, and three points for every first prize won in a breed class at a championship show. At an open show, three or more dogs must be entered and present in a class for a point to be claimed. A form on which to apply for the Junior Warrant can be obtained from The Kennel Club's Awards Department. This must be filled in correctly, giving details of the shows, with dates and classes, for which the points are claimed. When completed, the form must be returned to The Kennel Club, and you will subsequently receive a Junior Warrant certificate and a Stud Book number for the dog.

Affixes

If your show specimen is a bitch and you are successful with her you may decide to breed from her. In this case, your may want to register an *affix*, usually referred to as a *kennel name*. The Kennel Club will supply a form on which to apply to register an affix, and you are required to offer several words. This is in case you choose one that is already registered, one to which someone objects (the names are listed in *The Kennel Gazette* so that people may raise objections if the name is too close to their own) or one of which The Kennel Club does not approve. At the time of writing, the cost of registering an affix is £45 and there is an annual upkeep fee.

The granting of an affix entitles you to register any litters with your own kennel name, using it as a *prefix*, that is *before* the chosen name for each dog. For instance, if your chosen kennel name is *Blankton*, and it is accepted, you may then register the dogs as say

Blankton Bob, *Blankton Bijou* and so on. You may not register any of the puppies as, say, *Betty of Blankton*.

If, however, you buy in a registered dog (for instance *Acrelands Topsy*), you are permitted to add your own kennel name as a *suffix*, that is *after* the registered name (for instance, *Acrelands Topsy of Blankton*). Instead of *of Blankton*, it is permissible to use such forms as *from Blankton*, *to Blankton* or *at Blankton*.

Unless you are serious about staying in the world of dog showing and becoming a breeder, it is rather a waste of money to register an affix.

General Advice

As you progress in the dog world you will find many more forms to be filled in. The same advice is given for all: read the instructions carefully and follow them, always use block capitals, do not forget to sign forms, check all forms thoroughly before posting and do not leave anything until the last minute, as that is when mistakes are likely to occur. It is quite useful to take photocopies of all forms and file them.

With the increasing use of computers and the advances in office technology, the rules for entering dogs at shows may change. At the time of writing The Kennel Club is considering the feasibility of issuing standard entry forms. It is essential to read the dog press to keep up with any changes.

In fact, the rules for showing dogs are changing constantly. Those given in this book are correct at the time of writing (Spring 1998) but are subject to alteration by The Kennel Club at any time. The exhibitor must study the dog press constantly to be up to date and ready to comply with any changes.

First Steps in the Ring

The time has come to take your first steps in the ring. When judging, I have had new exhibitors showing under me who are so nervous that their hands are shaking and the perspiration is running down their faces. This is not good, as your nervous state will be transmitted to the dog, who will also become apprehensive and not give of its best.

Try to relax before your class. A cup of hot tea or coffee helps (not strong drink!), as does taking several really deep breaths before going into the ring. Think of the dog, not of yourself; it is the dog that is going to be judged, not you. It helps to be comfortably and neatly dressed and to wear well fitting shoes.

Ring Numbers

All exhibitors have to wear a ring number. Each dog is given a number for the day and has only one number for all its classes. These numbers are printed on squares of cardboard and must be worn by the exhibitor when entering the ring. They can be attached to the coat or shirt by ring clips, obtainable quite cheaply from stands selling dog equipment, pinned on, or attached to the upper arm by a rubber band. A recent invention is a card holder mounted on velcro that fits around the arm and holds itself in place.

At limited shows the numbers often have to be collected from a table inside the door. At some of these and at all open shows the ring numbers are given out to exhibitors as they enter the ring for their classes. At most championship shows ring numbers are left on the benches and correspond with the numbers slotted into the wire frames above each bench. However, at some championship and breed shows the numbers are obtainable in the ring, so do not panic if you do not find the number on your bench.

In the Ring

Once you are in the ring the steward will indicate where you have to stand. Do not take your place at the head of the line-up – try to get in further down so that you can watch what other exhibitors do before your turn comes.

First, the judge will walk down the line of dogs and look at them from a short distance to determine the make and shape of the entry. You should have your dog standing correctly while this is happening.

The judge will then indicate that he or she requires the dogs to be trotted all together around the ring. Keep up with the pace; do not lag behind or try to over-run the person in front. As with driving, it is correct to keep a distance between yourself and the person in front.

Some judges send the exhibitors around the ring twice or more. The more experienced judge is usually content with one circle unless this is ragged, in which case the dogs will be sent around once more. The line halts where it began.

Next, the first dog in line is called into the centre of the ring or, if it is a small breed, placed on the table for individual examination, and then moved. While this is going on, allow your dog to relax; it is not necessary to alert it to the job until the dog immediately in front of you is being examined. Now get your dog ready for its turn. If you try to keep your dog standing in show position all through the judging you will just weary it and it will go slack and become bored and inattentive.

Do watch what the judge is doing and how he instructs the other exhibitors. Notice if he asks for the dogs to be moved firstly in a triangle and then up and down or if he just wants the up and down movement twice. To know what you will be asked to do relieves the tension.

When your turn comes, take your dog out confidently and stand it up. Do not fuss – just get it standing and keeping still. No judge can see a dog if the exhibitor's hands are all over it, adjusting legs and so on. If you are showing a coated breed and take your brush into the ring, leave the brush on the table when the judge is examining your dog and do not groom it while the examination is taking place.

If you are showing one of the breeds that is put on a table for the judge to go over (referred to as *table dogs*) you may put your dog on the table as soon as the dog ahead has been seen and removed to show its paces. This allows you ample time to get your dog standing nicely for when the judge turns to look at it.

Incorrectly presented. The show slip is too tight, the dog's head is at the wrong angle and the mouth is open. Photo: Robert Smith

When the time comes to move the dog, see that the slip lead is in the correct position, speak to the dog and move off in a confident manner, completing the exercise as directed by the judge. When you have moved the dog, halt a few paces from the judge and let the dog stand naturally.

All judges have their own methods, so pay particular attention to what the judge does and what he or she tells you to do, and follow the directions.

Some judges just require you to move your dog in a triangle, and it is essential that you have mastered the art of walking a triangle at home when practising with your dog. Some judges just send the dog twice up and down the ring, stepping to one side to see the dog in profiles. Keep an eye on the judge to see where he or she is standing

Correctly presented. Slip lying free on shoulder, exhibitor's hand discreetly placed behind dog's head, dog alert and standing naturally. Photo: Robert Smith

if judging is carried out in this fashion and make sure the dog is always on the judge's side so that it can be seen. It is amazing how many exhibitors fail to do this, so that all the judge sees are the exhibitor's legs. It is vital to train your dog to stand facing either way when posed and to move on either side of the handler.

Once the judge has seen all the dogs individually he or she will size up the line and then pull out the choices. Some judges pull out and place straight away; some, especially if it is a large class, pull out five or six, send the others out and then take a further look at their selection, possibly moving them again before placing them. Again, follow the judge's instructions.

The chosen dogs are then lined up in the centre of the ring, in order one to five from the left. Both steward and judge will note

Moving the Dog to its Best Advantage

1 When moving, get the dog into the correct stride for the breed and keep the same pace. This dog is striding out well; the lead is not tight, but the handler has good control.

2 This handler has the dog in a tight grip. The front feet are off the floor and the dog's movement is severely restricted.

3 Move the dog in a
   straight line away
   from the judge

4 Bring the dog in a
   straight line back to
   the judge.

5 When moving,
   keep the dog
   between yourself
   and the judge.

6 The wrong way.
   The handler is between
   the dog and the judge, so
   the dog's topline and
   side movement cannot be
   properly evaluated.

Photos: Frank Naylor
Models: Marisa Keophaithool
and 'Jed'

down the numbers of the five placed, and then the steward will hand out the prize cards. If you are one of the lucky ones, do not leave the line-up until told you may do so.

The judge writes a critique of the first prize-winner in each class at open shows and the first and second at championship shows. This is why you must not leave the line-up until directed if you are in this enviable position, as the judge will be making notes on the placed dogs. At Crufts the first three places get a write-up.

Basset Hounds are long and low and look better if the handler is on a level.
Photo: Robert Smith

Ring Etiquette

Etiquette is rather an old-fashioned word nowadays, but it still exists in the show ring. Here are some 'dos' and 'do nots':

- *Do not* call judges by their first names while showing under them, however well you know them.
- *Do not* engage the judge in conversation.
- *Do not* smoke in the ring.

- *Do not* chat to ringsiders, or try to sort out some family problem that has arisen at the ringside; it doesn't look good.
- *Do not* chatter too much. Although you may speak to the exhibitors either side of you, you are all there to show your dogs, so your attention should be on this.
- *Do not* carry your handbag around the ring while showing your dog. Some lady exhibitors bring their handbags into the ring, wisely not liking to leave them on their bench or by the ring. It is in order to ask the steward if you may leave the bag under the judge's table, a favour always granted.
- *Do not* engage in criticism of the judge, the judging or the placed dogs when you leave the ring. This can lead to bad feeling, stop you making friends and advertise your ignorance as a newcomer.
- *Do* smile cheerfully if you are not placed. A good loser is appreciated.
- *Do* win gracefully if you are placed, without getting puffed up or complacent.

There is nothing like dog showing for experiencing ups and downs. All judges have their own priorities, and a dog that wins one week can equally well be at the bottom of the pile the following week. It is the vagaries of judging that keep the show scene rolling merrily along for, if the same dogs always won, the whole thing would grind to a halt.

No perfect dog has yet been bred, although some have come close to perfection. Perhaps we must hope that we never learn how to clone the best; if we did, there would be little point in showing.

Cups and Trophies

If you are lucky enough to win a trophy, you collect it from the cup steward's table and usually have to sign for it and possibly pay a small fee (50p or £1) towards insurance. Please keep trophies and cups clean and be sure to return them when requested, possibly at the next show.

Coping With Problems

Nothing worthwhile is ever accomplished unless one accepts that sometimes the path will be rocky and that there will be hazards and difficulties to overcome. The hazards in dog showing are many and varied; some, for the newcomer, are nerve-wracking.

'Relief' in the Ring

You are just taking your dog at a smart pace down the ring when it squats down to relieve itself.

This can usually be avoided by giving it an opportunity to empty itself in the exercise area before entering the ring. However, some dogs hate 'going' at shows and hold on until they are so full that they have to squat and leave a pool or a heap. It is embarrassing, but not unusual.

When this occurs during an individual show the judge will often go on to the next exhibit while your dog finishes its job and you and the steward clean up. Usually the judge will return to your dog later and give it a chance to show without interruption.

If your dog relieves itself when standing in the line or circling the ring with the others, it is up to you to clean up. In this case, another exhibitor will always hold your dog while you go for the bucket and shovel, and the steward will also be on hand to assist.

If a dog relieves itself in the centre of the ring it is amazing how stupid some exhibitors are. When they show their own dogs, they take a track over the soiled patch, which means that their own dog automatically slows down and tries to sniff. If there is such a patch when you are exhibiting, take your dog on a track well away from it so that it will not be distracted.

The Refusal

Sometimes a dog will get half way down the mat and stick its toes in, utterly refusing to go any further. However well you have taught your dog to show, this can happen. Apart from sheer bloody-mindedness, the causes can be many and varied.

Someone may have used a flash at the ringside, or there may be a loud crash outside the ring. Equally, a small child could run into the ring. Any of these things could startle the dog and cause it to lose concentration.

A male dog may have caught wind of a bitch about to come into season or coming out of it, whereupon all reason departs. I used to have a stud dog like this, and great tact had to be used to get him moving again.

The gadget you are using for leading the dog may be causing discomfort – in fact this is the most usual cause of the sudden stop. At the time of writing, many exhibitors opt for a choke lead or chain. This is a single cord, leather, nylon or chain threaded through a metal ring (called a *running slip*), and it pulls tightly around the dog's throat, causing it acute discomfort and often making it choke and retch. A dog in such discomfort might get frightened and decide not to cooperate – and who could blame it? If you go down on all fours and get someone to suspend *you* on a running slip, as it tightens around your throat like a vice you will understand how the dog feels. Slip leads and chains should always be self-adjusting so that the pressure can slacken and there is no tight constriction around the throat.

So many exhibitors string their dogs (of all breeds) up so tightly on the move that sometimes the dogs' front feet hardly touch the ground. Dogs should be trained to show on loose leads; that way the dog will be comfortable and not fight the handler either by pulling backwards, forwards or sideways or by refusing to move at all. Dogs shown on loose leads balance themselves more naturally, so their weight will be more evenly distributed on their four feet. They will therefore move better and more easily and achieve more drive from the rear.

If your dog comes to a grinding halt, do not stand in front and pull it; it will never move at all. Waving food in its face won't help either. Go back to its side, look straight ahead, give it a pat and an encouraging word, slacken the lead, and step forward. In most cases, the dog will go with you but, if you look down or behind you or pull the lead tight, forward progress will stop immediately.

If you have a small dog, pick it up and go to the end of the ring to see if it will walk towards the judge. If it does, keep going and turn the corner at the same pace when you reach the judge, hoping that the dog will walk back down the ring. Sometimes this works well; sometimes you have a stubborn dog that wants its own way. Do not engage in a battle of wills in the centre of the ring. If the dog is resolute, lift it to the side of the ring and apologise to the judge, who can then proceed with the next dog.

A judge who likes your dog will quite possibly come back to you when he or she has seen all the others, giving you another chance. If this happens, *do not* take your dog over the spot where it refused last time. Choose another track down the ring.

Nose to the Ground

Another hazard, particularly in outside rings, is the enticing smells in the grass that make it difficult to keep the dog's nose off the ground. Deal with this by placing the slip lead under the jaw bone and behind the ears, keeping it taut but not too taut. Give the dog an encouraging word and a cheerful chuck under the chin and walk along sharply. Sometimes you will be successful; sometimes nothing will do any good. On one occasion when spaniels were being shown at a big championship show, the rings were set out in an area previously occupied by pheasant rearing pens. I don't think any spaniel raised its nose from the ground that day – they were transfixed by the smell of birds!

Aggression

Dogs that back off from the judge, snarl, growl or even try to bite cannot be judged and the judge may ask the exhibitor to remove such a dog from the ring. However, as I pointed out in an earlier chapter, if you have a dog with a temperament problem, *do not attempt to show it*.

Indoor Hazards

There is a world of difference between showing inside and outside. At winter shows all judging takes place indoors, and you will find yourself in a variety of venues as your showing career unfolds. There will be small village halls, larger village halls, halls with very slippery floors, halls marked out in brilliant paint for ball games, and often two rings where only one can reasonably be accommodated.

Most societies provide strips of rubber matting around the perimeter and down the centre of the ring of place in a triangular shape. These are for the dogs to walk on. It is extraordinary how many exhibitors, usually new to the job, walk on the mats and leave their dogs to slip and slide on the polished floor. Do wear shoes with non-slip soles, as it is you who will have to negotiate the corners while your dog keeps to the matting.

Bright lines on floors alarm some dogs. If you see that the hall is so set out, try to get your dog to look at these and walk over them before its class. Sports centres are the venues for many large open shows with the dogs being shown in the games hall of these, so there are always coloured lines there.

At the big championship shows the halls are very large. Rings at these shows are usually large enough for the dogs to be moved freely. At Crufts the rings are covered by green carpeting.

All outdoor shows have to provide indoor rings as well in case of bad weather. When attending an outdoor show in the rain, or if it looks like rain, find out where your wet weather tent is as soon as you arrive. This will save a panic if you hear your breed called and do not know where to go.

Some undercover rings are very small and inadequate, and sometimes the ground is very uneven. Often there is a tent pole in the ring. However, the bigger championship shows now use the new 'in and out' marquees, which are a big improvement.

Outdoor Hazards

In fine weather there is nothing like showing off your dog in the sun. All breeds look their best on green grass with the sun shining on them, and most show best on grass.

The rings at some open shows are not well prepared and may be rough or uneven, while those at most championship shows will have been mown. As most show grounds are grazed when not in use for shows, sheep and cattle droppings can also be a problem – the dogs find them rivetting!

Take a good look around the ring while waiting your turn. Note

any dips and hollows and take care that neither end of your dog is set up in one of these, as the outline will then be spoiled. Choose a flat piece of ground for this purpose.

Some outdoor shows are held on grounds where there are thistles. These can get into dogs' feet, especially if the ground has

On hot days, put a wet towel over the dog's back to keep it cool.
Photo: Robert Smith

been mown and they have dried. If you are in this sort of ring, check your dog to make sure it has not picked up a sharp piece of thistle in its foot; if it has, it may go lame.

Showing your dog outside in a strong wind can be a hazard if you have a heavy-coated breed. This is one time when you *will* need your brush in the ring. Try to keep the dog's head turned into the wind; if you turn its backside into the wind the coat will blow inside out and the dog will start to shiver.

In a very cold wind, take a small rug into the ring and put this over the dog's back while waiting to be judged. This is particularly necessary if you have a smooth-coated breed such as a Pointer or a Whippet. Toy dogs such as English Toy Terriers or Chihuahuas can be picked up and popped inside exhibitors' coats.

In very hot weather, soak a towel in cold water, wring it out well and take it with you into the ring. It can be placed over the dog's head and back as it waits for its turn. You can leave the towel at the ringside when the dog is being seen and retrieve it when you return to the line. Try to stand between the sun and the dog to make a shade for it.

Dogs pant heavily in hot weather and there have been all sorts of suggestions for stopping them. The line of the head is altered if the dog's mouth is wide open and the tongue hanging out. However, panting helps the dog to fend off excessive heat, so it is unwise to stop it for long. Carry in your pocket a small cloth soaked in cold water, wrung out and sprinkled with lemon juice. Just before the judge examines your dog, wipe its mouth out with the cooling cloth.

If you are showing one of the dribbling breeds such as a St Bernard or a Newfoundland, take a towel into the ring. This can be draped around the dog's neck like a bib while you are waiting your turn to prevent the coat on the chest from becoming wet and spoiling the dog's appearance.

Usually, Bull breeds and Chow Chows are judged under cover in very hot weather as they suffer greatly in a heat wave. If you are showing one of these breeds it is a good idea to travel with a container of ice, which can be applied to the dog if it appears to be affected. This can often happen in the car on the way to the show, especially if you are held up in traffic. Incidentally, a veterinary surgeon should always be summoned if a dog appears to be suffering from heat stroke.

You may be happily engaged in showing your dog in an outside ring when a storm breaks and the rain pours down. The steward will know the shortest way to the wet weather ring, so follow him or her. Some judges prefer to finish their judging in the rain rather than break their concentration. If weather conditions are doubtful it is as well to take a raincoat to the ringside as well as something to cover the dog if necessary.

Arriving Late

The biggest nightmare for the dog exhibitor is arriving late at a show. This may be for any number of reasons: failure to start early enough, a breakdown, a traffic jam, and so on. You arrive panting and distraught at the ringside – only to find that your class is just over. It is probably the most disappointing moment of your life.

Can your transfer to another class? No, if you miss your class, for whatever reason, that is the end of the day's showing. Try to put on a brave face – it's happened to all of us.

Sometimes you arrive late and your class is just going into the ring. You hurtle in, dog uncombed and you panting and panic-stricken. Take your place at the end of the line. This gives you time to run a brush over the dog, get your breath and prepare to give a polished performance when the judge calls you out. Do not chatter to other exhibitors about your failure to arrive early. Just concentrate on getting calm enough to give your dog every chance. You can tell anyone who will listen the story of your misfortunes on the road when you are safely out of the ring.

Late arrivals should catch the eye of the steward before entering the ring and enquire whether they may join the class. The steward then asks the judge, and most will let you in if they have not yet started to pick their winners. It is impolite to rush into a class that is halfway through; always see the steward before entering the ring. There is no need to apologise to the judge as long as you are accepted into the class. Apologies are not really necessary and could come under the heading of unnecessary conversations with the judge.

Do not, please, ever question the judge. The judge's decision is final and whether you agree with his or her findings is neither here nor there.

Show Slips

1 The running noose. Not advised for novice handlers as, in the wrong hands or with an untrained dog, it can act as a garotte.

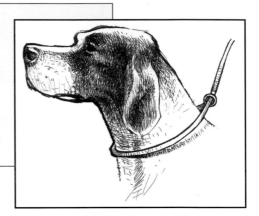

2 Adjustable slip. Can be obtained in several materials. The keeper (A) can be run up or down the slip by the handler to obtain the desired fitting. Very suitable for small or toy breeds, but...

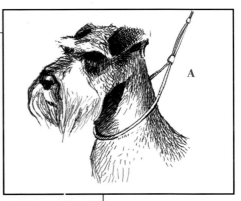

3 ... on larger breeds an ill-fitting slip can result in the dog escaping in the ring.

4 Smooth Collies Southcombe Saffron and Foxearth Absolutely Fab for Antoc model the self-adjusting slip, composed of a leather neckpiece and light chain. This is ideal as it gives the handler correct control and is comfortable for the dog. Photos: Bill Welsh.

5 The Border Terrier Minnihaha of Westacres models the self-adjusting leather slip, which comes in all sizes. Photos: Robert Smith.

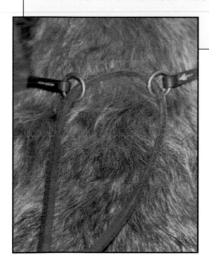

Questions and Answers

Can I join The Kennel Club?
No, The Kennel Club is a private members' club that was formed in 1873. Current membership numbers around 720. Members are elected as a result of being proposed and seconded by other members and having their names voted upon by the rest of the members.

There is an associate membership for which people can apply. If they are accepted, they must pay a yearly subscription. The elected associate does not have the rights of full membership.

What does The Kennel Club do?
The Kennel Club holds a monopoly in the world of pedigree dogs in Great Britain. Before any dog can be shown it has to be registered, and this can only be done through The Kennel Club.

No dog show can be held without a licence issued by The Kennel Club. Any judge officiating at an unlicensed show can be banned from judging at Kennel Club licensed shows.

The Kennel Club has many rules governing all aspects of the pedigree dog scene, from shows to judges, from the behaviour of dogs to that of people. Anyone flouting any of the rules can be summoned to appear before a Kennel Club tribunal and, if found guilty of the offence, be fined or, in an extreme case, banned for a term of years or even life from judging, showing or both.

The Kennel Club also checks all wins and can disqualify any dog wrongly entered or winning an award for which it is not eligible. Winning dogs bred by the judge will be disqualified.

Does The Kennel Club have a magazine that anyone can purchase?
Yes, the *Kennel Gazette* is printed monthly. It is available by post and at time of writing costs £2 an issue.

Does the Kennel Gazette *give details of dogs that have been registered?*
No. In past years all this information was printed in the monthly

Kennel Gazette, but the volume of dogs registered, transferred and exported has become so vast that separate, quarterly publications are issued. For details of these *Breed Record Supplements*, which cost £2 each and are divided into groups, and to order them and/or the *Kennel Gazette*, contact: Publications Department, The Kennel CLub, 1 Clarges Street, London W1Y 8AB.

How do I go about registering a dog?
You can only register a dog if you have bred it. Forms are available from The Kennel Club Registration Department. If you buy a dog and it is not registered you must contact the breeder and ask him or her to register it. You may then transfer the dog to your name.

It is unwise to buy an unregistered dog if you are keen to show it. Both the breeder and the owner of its sire will have to sign the registration form and, if either of them cannot be contacted, the dog will remain unregistered.

Always buy stock from an established kennel. When you collect your puppy you should be given the pedigree, registration certificate (the transfer portion of which will be signed by the breeder), a diet sheet and, if the puppy's been inoculated, a vaccination record book. Many breeders also give information about how the puppy has been reared and suggestions for its future welfare. Some litters are insured by the breeder, in which case the papers for your puppy will include the policy.

What do I do next?
As advised in chapter 7 of this book, transfer the puppy to your name. Keep all the puppy's papers together in a file. Once the puppy has been fully inoculated it should have boosters each year. When you take the dog to have this done, take the vaccination record book with you, and the veterinary surgeon will record the date of the booster. Most surgeries send reminders each year to their clients but, if you move to another district, the note in this book will remind you when the dog is due for its next annual booster.

Against what do the inoculations guard?
Distemper, Parvovirus, Hepatitis and Leptospirosis.

What is HD?

Hip Dysplasia, which in recent years has been found to affect some breeds. Check whether your breed is subject to HD and what scheme is run by the breed club for screening and scoring.

What is PRA?

Progressive Retinal Atrophy, a condition affecting certain breeds and causing blindness when dogs get older. Clubs for various breeds have schemes for checking eyes.

What is a Challenge Certificate (CC)?

Challenge Certificates (CCs) are awarded by The Kennel Club, which decides each year how many sets will be allocated to each breed for the following year.

Challenge Certificates are awarded to the Best Dog and Best Bitch from winners of the classes at championship shows in which the breed has been allocated a set of CCs by The Kennel Club. There are also Reserve Challenge Certificates for the second best dog and bitch. If the winner of either CC is disqualified, the winner of the Reserve will be given the CC. If either CC is withheld by the judge because he or she does not consider the entrant of good enough quality to receive one, the Reserve CC must also be withheld.

How is a champion made?

To become a champion a dog must win three CCs at championship shows under three different judges. For gundog breeds and Border Collies, dogs that have won three CCs are styled *show champions* and can only become champions if they also win a Working Test (for Border Collies) or a Working Certificate at a show gundog field day or a Field Trial (for gundog breeds).

What do the letters NAF and TAF stand for?

NAF stands for *Name Applied For* and is used by the owners who have added their affixes to an existing name but not received notification from The Kennel Club that the name has been accepted before the closing date for the show.

TAF stands for *Transfer Applied For* and is added to a dog's name when transfer of ownership has been applied for but the transfer has not been received from The Kennel Club before the closing date of entries.

Do I have to handle my dog in the ring myself or can someone else do so?
There is no rule that says you must handle your own dog. Anyone can show the dog at your direction.

What is a professional handler?
A professional handler is someone who takes other people's dogs, conditions and trains them and handles them in the ring. There is a scale of charges for this service. In Great Britain there have always been a few professional handlers but in other countries, notably the United States of America, most of the handling is done by professionals.

What is a Stud Book number?
Each year The Kennel Club publishes a *Stud Book* in which are recorded the names and details of dogs and bitches who have won or been placed in designated classes at championship shows during the previous year. These are then given a Stud Book number. Dogs and bitches to whom a Stud Book number has already been allocated for wins in previous years but who have won in the preceding year are also noted, although their details are not again given in full. Stud book numbers have always been a measure of the worth of a dog, as it is assumed that only good dogs get into the *Stud Book*. The first *Stud Book* was published in 1874. From 1998 dogs winning Junior Warrants will have Stud Book numbers allocated to them.

You do not have to apply to have your dog registered in the *Stud Book*; this is done automatically by The Kennel Club.

If I am at a show and wish to complain about the action of a fellow exhibitor or the treatment of a dog, what do I do?
To lodge a complaint you must first get someone to stand as a witness to the scene. You then report the incident to the secretary, put down a fee of £35 and give your name and address and that of your witness or witnesses. The complaint will be investigated and, if it is allowed, your £35 will be returned. If the complaint is deemed

Showing Dogs Outside

Choose a flat surface in the ring. Most outside rings have bumps and dips. Dogs standing in them present unbalanced outlines.

Wrong The dog's back feet are in a dip.

Wrong The dog's front feet are in a dip.

Correct The handler has chosen a level patch and the dog is now standing balanced.

Wrong Windy days are difficult for exhibitors of long-coated breeds. It is better to stand the dog head on to the wind: otherwise, this can happen!

frivolous, you will lose your deposit. Be warned that, although at the time people will say they will be witnesses, when it comes to the crunch many, sometimes all, pull out, leaving you with no case and the loss of your deposit. Complaints should only be made in serious cases of offense; actual bodily violence or physical abuse of a dog or dogs.

The procedure is the same if you wish to lodge an objection to a dog you think has been wrongly entered or against a fellow exhibitor who you think has transgressed the rules.

New exhibitors should not make complaints if they can help it as they do not yet know all the rules that govern the dog scene and may find themselves unpopular.

A word of warning: in the world of dogs, as in any other walk of life, there are a few professional troublemakers. Do be careful not to get embroiled with them or you may find you are left to fire the bullets they have loaded. Then, if things go wrong, you are the one in the hot seat who takes all the blame while those who instigated the complaint or objection, for which you may later find there were no grounds, are long gone.

What is the Import Register?
A new breed entering the country is put on the Import Register. There will be no classes especially for the breed: it has to compete with all the other newly-imported breeds.

What is the Rare Breeds Register?
When a new breed has been in the country for several years and numbers have been built up to the desired level, The Kennel Club removes the breed from the import register and places it on the Rare Breeds Register. Classes may be offered for individual rare breeds.

Do Import and Rare Breeds compete for Challenge Certificates?
No, no CCs are allocated to breeds on these registers. Usually when a breed has been on the Rare Breeds Register for 10 years or more, the numbers of generations bred will be considered by The Kennel Club and, if they are deemed suitable, the breed will then be taken off the Rare Breeds Register and CCs will be allocated to it.

Groups

Dog breeds are divided into seven groups, and these groups with their members are listed below. Against some will be seen the word [Interim], indicating that there are not yet enough of the breed for a Challenge Certificate allocation.

Hound Group

Aghan Hound
Basenji
Basset Fauve de Bretagne [Interim]
Basset Hound
Beagle
Bloodhound
Borzoi
Dachshunds
Deerhound
Elkhound
Finnish Spitz
Foxhound [Interim]
Grand Basset Griffon Vendéen
    [Interim]
Grand Bleu de Gascoigne [Interim]
Greyhound
Hamiltonstovare [Interim]
Ibizan Hound
Irish Wolfhound
Norwegian Lundehund [Interim]
Otterhound
Petit Basset Griffon Vendéen
Pharaoh Hound
Rhodesian Ridgeback
Saluki
Segugio Italiano [Interim]
Sloughi [Interim]
Whippet

Terrier Group

Airedale Terrier
Australian Terrier
Bedlington Terrier
Border Terrier
Bull Terriers
Cairn Terrier
Cesky Terrier [Interim]
Dandie Dinmont Terrier
Fox Terrier (Smooth)
Fox Terrier (Wire)
Glen of Imaal Terrier [Interim]
Irish Terrier
Kerry Blue Terrier
Lakeland Terrier
Manchester Terrier
Norfolk Terrier
Norwich Terrier
Parson Jack Russell Terrier
Scottish Terrier
Sealyham Terrier
Skye Terrier
Soft Coated Wheaten Terrier
Staffordshire Bull Terrier
Welsh Terrier
West Highland White Terrier

Working Group

Alaskan Malamute (Interim)
Beauceron
Bernese Mountain Dog
Bouvier des Flandres
Boxer
Bullmastiff
Continental Landseer
Dobermann
Eskimo Dog [Interim]
Giant Schnauzer
Great Dane
Leonberger
Mastiff
Neapolitan Mastiff [Interim]
Newfoundland
Pinscher [Interim]
Portuguese Water Dog [Interim]
Rottweiler
St Bernard
Siberian Husky
Tibetan Mastiff [Interim]

Pastoral Group

Anatolian Shepherd Dog [Interim]
Australian Cattle Dog [Interim]
Australian Shepherd Dog
Bearded Collie
Belgian Shepherd Dog
Bergamasco [Interim]
Border Collie
Briard
Collie (Rough)
Collie (Smooth)
Estrela Mountain Dog [Interim]
Finnish Lapphund [Interim]
German Shepherd Dog (Alsatian)
Hovawart [Interim]
Hungarian Kuvasz [Interim]
Hungarian Puli
Komondor [Interim]
Lancashire Heeler [Interim]
Maremma Sheepdog

Norwegian Buhund
Old English Sheepdog
Polish Lowland Sheepdog [Interim]
Pyrenean Mountain Dog
Pyrenean Sheepdog [Interim]
Samoyed
Shetland Sheepdog
Swedish Lapphund [Interim]
Swedish Valhund
Welsh Corgi (Cardigan)
Welsh Corgi (Pembroke)

Gundog Group

Bracco Italiano [Interim]
Brittany
English Setter
German Shorthaired Pointer
German Wirehaired Pointer
Gordon Setter
Hungarian Vizsla
Hungarian Wirehaired Vizsla [Interim]
Irish Red and White Setter
Irish Setter
Italian Spinone
Kooikerhondje [Interim]
Large Munsterlander
Nova Scotia Duck Tolling Retriever
    [Interim]
Pointer
Retriever (Chesapeake Bay) [Interim]
Retriever (Curly Coated)
Retriever (Flat Coated)
Retriever (Golden)
Retriever (Labrador)
Spaniel (American Cocker)
Spaniel (Clumber)
Spaniel (Cocker)
Spaniel (English Springer)
Spaniel (Field)
Spaniel (Irish Water)
Spaniel (Sussex)
Spaniel (Welsh Springer)
Weimaraner

Utility Group

Boston Terrier
Bulldog
Canaan Dog [Interim]
Chow Chow
Dalmatian
French Bulldog
German Spitz
Japanese Akita
Japanese Shiba Inu
Japanese Spitz
Keeshond
Lhasa Apso
Miniature Schnauzer
Poodles
Schipperke
Schnauzer
Shar Pei [Interim]
Shih Tzu
Tibetan Spaniel
Tibetan Terrier

Toy Group

Affenpinscher
Australian Silky Terrier [Interim]
Bichon Frisé
Bolognese [Interim]
Cavalier King Charles Spaniel
Chihuahua
Chinese Crested Dog
Coton de Tulear [Interim]
English Toy Terrier (Black and Tan)
Griffon Bruxellois
Italian Greyhound
Japanese Chin
King Charles Spaniel
Lowchen (Little Lion Dog)
Maltese
Miniature Pinscher
Papillon
Pekingese
Pomeranian
Pug
Yorkshire Terrier

New breeds are constantly being imported from overseas so, by the time this book is published, there may be other breeds to add to these groups.

Useful Addresses

The Kennel Club
1–5 Clarges Street
Piccadilly
London   W1Y 8AB
Tel: 0171 493 2001

Dog World
Somerfield House
Wotton Road
Ashford
Kent   TN23 6LW
Fax: 01233 645669

Weekly dog paper published Fridays.

Our Dogs
Oxford Road
Station Approach
Manchester   M60 1SX
Tel: 0161 2281984

Weekly dog paper published Fridays.

National Tattoo Register
Registrar: Mr R A Frost
Trenarren
Mersea Road
Langenhoe
Colchester
Essex   CO5 7II
Tel: 01206 735336

A tried and tested method of identifying dogs. Useful if the dog is lost or stolen. Permanent identification.

Ministry of Agriculture
Freephone on poisons: 0180 032 1600
Information about poisons that can affect dogs.

Animal Health Trust
PO Box 5
Newmarket
Suffolk   CB8 7DW
Tel: 01638 661111

Council for Docked Breeds
Secretary: Ginette Elliott
Marlsburg Kennels
Whitehall Lane
Thorpe-Le-Soken
Essex   CO11 0AP
Tel: 01255 830993

Ryslip Kennels
Binfield Park
Bracknell
Berks
Tel: 0134 442 4144

Should you have to move overseas and wish to take your dogs, Ryslip will attend to travel details and documents and supply travelling crates. Should you wish to import a dog from overseas, Ryslip also has a quarantine kennel.

Index